I0102271

Other novellas by Greg Cornwell:

1. *Order and the Abandoned Body*

2. *Order and the Merimbula Mystery*

3. *Order and the Luckless Lovers*

4. *Order and the Parliamentary Conference*

5. *Order and the Motel Murder*

TWILIGHT

- A Nursing Home Mystery -

GREG CORNWELL

Copyright © 2019 Greg Cornwell

ISBN: 978-1-925952-24-7
Published by Vivid Publishing
A division of Fontaine Publishing Group
P.O. Box 948, Fremantle
Western Australia 6959
www.vividpublishing.com.au

A catalogue record for this
book is available from the
National Library of Australia

All rights reserved. This is a work of fiction. Names, characters, businesses, places, events and incidents are either the products of the author's imagination or used in a fictitious manner. Any resemblance to actual persons, living or dead, or actual events is purely coincidental. No part of this publication may be reproduced, stored in a retrieval system or transmitted in any form or by any means, electronic, mechanical, photocopying, recording or otherwise, without the prior written permission of the copyright holder.

To those who suffered and to those who still suffer

PROLOGUE

I stood over her, shrunken in her bed, her face drawn and very thin, lines down it like a waterfall in the dry season, lips not so different from when they were pursed years earlier against one of my young misdemeanours.

I was about to stroke her hair, the alternative to kissing the narrow tight mouth which rarely opened for anything now, not even food.

Then I saw there was nothing much to stroke: a few wisps of grey which if scratched with a comb would probably scrape the balding head rather than adjust the hair – hair I remembered so rich of blonde colour, now reduced to these few scraps clinging to a decaying body.

My mother.

Lying there at the end of her life. A life of interest, of challenge, of success, and now this.

A hopelessly human wreck in a nursing home bed looked after, expensively, by nurses from predominantly African and Asian backgrounds who tried their best, but hampered by insufficient and inarticulate English were unable to adequately communicate with their patients.

In turn the patients often were unable to understand their gentle carers. Even for those hard of hearing written English was impossible, education had not advanced that far among the immigrants.

I heard a cry. Not close but locally, because most of the private room doors were open in case some mentally or physically crippled patient needed something, probably from their active past: a teddy bear, a lover's embrace, roses from the garden.

My mother was not like that. She was never one to make a scene, loudly demanding something, attention, affection …

Yet she knew what she wanted. Like this afternoon when in her rasping hardly audible voice and behind closed eyes, this aged ruin whispered she wanted to die, she'd had enough of life.

If love counted for anything …

I lifted the back of her skull with my gloved hand, removed the pillow it rested upon and placed it firmly over the old exhausted face.

Twilight Village hospital and nursing home covered a large entire block, appropriately on a quiet street opposite small comfortable country-style houses usually of wood with wide verandas in testimony to the summertime sun. One side where the actual nursing home was located looked across the street to a neglected park now principally wild bushland.

Twilight offered residents self-contained single storey units spread around a central dining room, the nursing home proper and a secure small dementia ward. Initially the nursing home was part of the main village hospital but increased demand as communities aged saw a major upward expansion of this section of the facility to three stories. The extra floors didn't matter because most of these bedridden patients weren't going anywhere else.

Logistics and more services required a separate operation, which began as a sub-group but increasingly became independent of the main village management, as was deemed necessary for this major aged complex of the prosperous farming district around the large rural centre of Drummond.

Cattle, crops and sheep, predominantly sheep, filled the open rolling hills and valleys of the surrounding countryside, whose elderly, it seemed from demand, welcomed the even expensive opportunity to live out their lives in such a familiar area.

This quiet pleasure and the bright spring morning outside the windows, with new buds festooning the shrubs and bushes, did not reflect the atmosphere inside the meeting room.

"The third in two months," confirmed Robert Carroll, Twilight Village management committee's representative to the nursing home's operations.

An ex-military officer, balding and running to fat, he typified such appointments, being there to chair meetings and to handle non-health issues, especially finance.

A local, he was dressed in the conventional country-style tweed jacket, check shirt and wool tie. His link to the land was through his elder brother who had inherited "Fairview" when their father died, but some complicated arrangement gave him shares.

He was respected in the district, however he was out-of-his-depth in this matter.

"They were all elderly," argued Reverend Andrew Lord, as if this justified the happenings.

Twilight Village had a vague association with local church groups and it had been thought prudent to recognise the fact, at least for those closest to the hereafter. He too was retired, a tall man perpetually stooped as often is the case with those seeking to be physically closer to those they wish to help. He wore a small identifying cross in his lapel.

"It's not the deaths, Andrew," Carroll said patiently. "It's the manner. Just stopped breathing. Look's suspicious."

"You're not suggesting my staff are somehow re-sponsible, Robert?" Matron Jarvis asked defensively and to head off objections from Shaun Wilson, the sandy haired young but committed union representa-tive with whom she had an often fragile relationship.

A stout woman, dark hair back in a bun, she demonstrated capability and a no-nonsense attitude.

"Of course not, Avril."

"Sister Connell and the night receptionist both report nothing untoward," the Matron continued, accompanied by vigorous nods from the two women in question who, not being members of the nursing home's committee, were sitting against the wall.

"No sign of struggles either," Jarvis added.

"That right, Doctor?"

V.J. Patel quietly agreed. An undemonstrative man of medium height and Indian origin, Dr Patel could have been described by the others present as over-dressed in his neat brown suit and matching tie, but he found his formality comforting in what was still a somewhat alien environment.

Strictly speaking he was not a member of the committee either, but as the home's visiting medical officer or VMO his presence around the building was so familiar he warranted inclusion on this ground alone. And someone needed to sign the paperwork for the deaths, suspicious or not.

"So there's nothing sinister to report?" Carroll said, with a meaningful look at Marion Turner, the government appointed hospital visitor.

Ms Turner, tall, middle-aged, with white to greying hair, was visitor to the entire hospital complex. Again, her presence because of such wider duties was not necessary, but Carroll and Matron Jarvis were cautious people, anxious to avoid any suggestion of a cover-up.

"Not that I can see, Robert," Marion Turner replied reassuringly.

"Could we ask Sister Connell to increase the night rounds?" asked Amy Bennett, the social worker. A rollie-polly figure of a woman, her kindly features suggested her destiny always was to be in social work.

"Would that really help?" wondered someone quietly as if not wishing to give offence.

"I agree," said Chairman Carroll, "an' there'd be possible extra staff costs to consider."

"Install security lights outside?" Amy Bennett tried again.

"And keep patients' awake?" Matron Jarvis said dismissively. "Not to mention the costs of installation and upkeep."

Not that it will make any difference if they double the security, I thought to myself, as the meeting broke up, the mystery unresolved.

D r V.J. Patel walked slowly and alone back to his office, little more than a small spare room, original purpose unknown, with a door, a chair and a bench at the back of the nursing home building on the ground floor. A window looked out upon the road and wild bushland opposite.

It was used irregularly for most of his visits were direct to elderly patients, but he welcomed the seclusion it provided for he still was an outsider.

Ironically the metropolis he worked in reminded him too readily of Mumbai and when the opportunity presented to move to this regional centre west of the mountains he accepted. No other Indian appeared to live here. He hadn't met any and, unlike the ubiquitous Chinese, there was no restaurant.

The nursing home was alright. The patients accepted the multicultural nursing staff even if they didn't understand them and the nursing staff accepted him as one of their own, albeit with respect. It was the upper echelons who still held him on probation and he was uneasily aware these patient deaths began only a month after he had taken up his position.

And despite the relaxed attitude publicly displayed by the Chairman, Dr Patel still sensed the doubt Robert Campbell harboured about the deaths being more than accidental.

Granted, elderly people dying in nursing homes was hardly unusual and particularly at the end of winter when pneumonia, once described to him as 'the old people's friend', did its compassionate work.

But the trio simply had stopped breathing. Nothing in his examinations suggested congested lungs or any other illness save old age itself. It was as if they'd been smothered.

Yet there was no evidence to support this allegation. The beds were undisturbed, each head lay peacefully upon its pillow and as far as he could remember the doors, although unlocked as required, had been closed like the others along the corridors. There was no pattern either about the locations: two were on the second floor, one on the third or top.

Nothing supported the vague suspicion something was wrong, however it was still there.

After the committee meeting I decided to suspend my healing activities for a spell. There was no urgency and some of the targets might take themselves off. Besides, an occurrence took place outside the nursing home which could indirectly benefit my efforts.

L arge as this regional centre was, Drummond still could not support a daily newspaper. It managed a publication twice a week, even running an occasional big story.

In this conservative rural heartland the story was big: a local couple Lois and Ben Blake, who had watched her aged mother die a painful, agonising death in a big city, had started a petition to legalise death with dignity and proposed a public meeting at the town hall where a prominent national advocate would speak.

Predictably the issue drew media comment with terms like euthanasia and mercy killing being introduced to prejudice the case, some people claimed, and divided the community.

The churches were inescapably involved.

The elderly local Catholic priest made it clear they were dealing with sin, wantonly taking a life no matter what the mental or physical condition of the patient and commended the excellent palliative care facilities available. The Anglican rector, the popular Brother Bob, was more circumspect, doubtless knowing the mixed views of his congregation, while the Uniting Church minister was out-of-town.

Believing the clergy well covered, parliamentary representatives were then approached for comment, with both Federal and State members agreeing to accept and submit the petition to their parliaments but would not be drawn on their personal position if the matter came before the House and a conscience vote was allowed – far too early, a rhetorical question.

The town council claimed it was outside its jurisdiction but the town hall was available to anyone wishing to hire it for a legitimate activity – which this proposed meeting was.

"Should we attend?" asked Amy Bennett, at another hastily convened committee meeting.

"Depends how you feel about euthanasia," said Matron Jarvis, perhaps betraying her position.

A silence followed around the table until Dr Patel said softly: "It might be difficult for Mrs Bennett not to attend as a social worker."

"A foot in both camps?" queried Marion Turner.

"Amy could attend," agreed Robert Carroll, "but it

might be awkward for some of the rest of us. Andrew and Avril, for example."

"And our staff?"

"No, Doctor," Matron Jarvis said emphatically, with a nod to Shaun Wilson. "No senior staff anyway. I don't want Twilight involved –"

"In case it happens again?" interrupted Marion Turner.

"Yes. If something *is* going on Twilight shouldn't be too closely associated with behaviour anathema to what we exist for."

"I shall attend," the union man stated. "It's in the interests of my members."

And perhaps their long-term jobs, thought V.J., while acknowledging the majority of Shaun Wilson's foreign workers needed an English-speaking advocate.

"Perhaps you could attend, Doctor, on our behalf?" Chairman Carroll suggested quickly, anticipating an argument between the staff representatives.

"You have professional experience of the subject," he added logically in the embarrassed silence which followed.

I don't really, thought Dr Patel. A doctor's job, black or white, Hippocratic Oath, is to protect lives wherever possible. Of course I haven't been here long, so I might not be as well-known as the rest of you. Handy if you wanted to shift any criticisms to a relative dark stranger.

"Yes, I could," V.J. agreed, recognising an opportunity to integrate himself favourably into the community with some slight risk from being a recent arrival and also to identifying locals, including Twilight staff, who might be sympathetic to the death with dignity cause. But he had to be careful of broader exposure.

"However," he added as Carroll smiled with relief, "I'll need a public explanation for my presence." Might as well spell out what everyone else at the table was hoping. "I don't want people thinking I'm there as a supporter of either side. Just an interested professional observer."

This was not what most of the committee wanted. The Chairman and Reverend Lord looked uncomfortable, Matron Jarvis looked sulky as if a scheme hadn't worked. Only Amy Bennett and Marion Turner held neutral expressions while Shaun Wilson looked into the distance.

"Maybe I should go," Robert Carroll decided reluctantly. "In an official capacity as chairman of this committee, you understand, to learn of possible ramifications for Twilight if this move becomes law."

Apart from an angry snort from the Matron, the committee was quick to agree. While nobody wanted the possibly suspicious deaths to become public, they all realised there was less risk to Twilight's reputation from a low-key fact finding attendance by its nursing home chairman – a local identity – than Dr Patel and his conditions.

Amy Bennet, instigator of the attendance discussion wasn't finished. She asked again about security.

"Outside security," she explained. "The doors into the nursing home building. Who has keys?"

"We all do, Amy," Robert Carroll explained. "Along with most of the few night staff. Sister Connell became tired of locking the doors after they arrived on duty so the dementia and insomniacs like Lady Jane Grey wouldn't wander out. Why?"

"I thought someone from outside might be getting in." The social worker at least was concerned about the deaths and earned an approving nod from Shaun Wilson.

"Highly unlikely, Amy, but it wouldn't be remiss to conduct a key check. See if anyone has lost or mislaid their copy. I'll ask Casey."

Listening to the show of concern around the table Dr Patel wondered who was lying. It's not those outside you need worry about, he thought, if there is anything to worry about it's here.

According to the local newspaper about 400 people attended the death with dignity meeting. The prominent national advocate provided a prejudiced but reasonable address and dealt effectively with the few hecklers while ignoring the *Life is Sacred* signs which greeted attendees upon arrival at the Drummond Town Hall. The crowd control police were bored.

Despite his reluctance to attend in any official capacity, Dr Patel was intrigued enough to join the several hundred others, sitting quietly at the back of the hall.

Neither as an Indian nor as a doctor had he given much thought to a person's free will to die, constantly surrounded as he was to usually avoidable death.

Thus the arguments in favour were confronting.

If homosexuality, miscegenation and slavery had

been faced and largely settled, claimed the prominent national advocate, as well as human rights against discrimination, racism, sexism and child labour to name a few, why did this taboo remain?

And the irony did not end there, with people offended at others elsewhere, especially children, shown on TV starving to death, yet allowing our own aged unwillingly to live.

He, for it was a man (which left V.J. wondering), criticised politicians for failure to address the issue while conceding their collective cautious nature, citing the time taken to recognise same-sex marriage.

Again to his credit contentious issues were approached head-on. Nursing homes, in the past subject to damning public enquiries, were a mixed bag from independent living to hostel and ultimately to dementia. However they were not cheap and not to everyone's taste, after a lifetime of privacy accommodated now in a communal aged boarding school.

The sensitive issue of reducing cost of care was dealt with by arguing a person who wanted to die faced with a grandchild whose life was at stake for financial reasons would unhesitatingly give way, while the hypocrisy of pumping people in pain full of drugs until they overdosed was again exposed.

Palliative care was not condemned, however statistics

were quoted not everyone believed it provided a 'good death', something better was needed and people should be able to choose.

The speaker concentrated his closing remarks upon the rights of the individual and how the person should be respected and not ignored like a child with a tantrum when they said they wanted to die. He highlighted the inequality of a wealthy person travelling overseas to somewhere death with dignity was permitted, while a pensioner was denied the financial opportunity to do so.

"Whatever happened to freedom of choice?" the speaker asked rhetorically, to scattered applause. "We need a national referendum!"

Dr Patel listened briefly to the early questions, that often began as speeches, and was disappointed some listeners still missed the point the matter concerned the sufferer and life at all costs or a diminished life was better than no life at all was promoted by the fit and healthy, if the appearance of the questioners was anything to go by.

Not wanting to be recognised by more people than necessary V.J. left the meeting early before the crowd, while the exchange continued now about overseas laws in place to protect those consenting to die from being provoked by avaricious relatives.

Next day Lois and Ben Blake were interviewed by regional television and by local radio – the prominent national advocate had left Drummond early that morning – and declared themselves pleased with the attendance and with the interest generated by the subject. They denied responsibility however for the small DWD with a red tick stickers which appeared upon hoardings, telegraph poles and some shop windows, thus incurring the wrath of the local council for vandalism.

Lois took part in a radio debate with a Monsignor from the Catholic Church's diocese, which largely centred on the success of palliative care, with the priest arguing its total success and Mrs Blake the contrary. A similar division of opinion occurred over the hypocrisy of drug overdosing for patients in extreme pain and over a person's right to decide whether or not they should live or die.

Standard arguments already canvassed in the death with dignity debate, agreed Dr Patel, endorsing the wisdom of the main Twilight Village board in declining the invitation for a representative of their nursing home section to participate.

Again it drew unnecessary attention to the Village with its still unpublicised recent deaths and also risked taking sides in what had become a sensitive if small-town local issue, if letters to the editor were judgements. Nonetheless the overall strategy proved successful. Robert Carroll's attendance at the meeting drew no public comment.

Only one matter caused the Doctor concern: the claim unscrupulous relatives would use any relaxation of the law to kill off their elderly for financial gain.

No lawyer himself, V.J. nevertheless believed it would be possible to enact legislation to protect the ill and the disabled from such greed, but in the absence of such legal restraints what if people simply were being murdered?

He reminded himself there was no evidence to support such suspicions over the Twilight Village deaths. Certainly there was no direct relationship between the three women who had died, although more detailed investigations could be carried out if necessary.

Even statistically there was nothing untoward: there were more women than men in nursing homes, so the mortality rate would be higher.

Another small issue, hardly worth considering, was Todd, Casey the nursing home night receptionist's boyfriend. Todd was rumoured to be politically ambitious and from the television footage had played a provocative role in the question time following the prominent national advocate's address at the town hall.

Todd strongly supported death with dignity and Casey had a key to all of the nursing homes outside doors.

The curiosity generated by the public meeting soon fell away however. The Drummond community might have found the subject initially challenging but more mundane and regular concerns returned: sheep and cattle prices, the weather, matters of their daily lives. Even the Blakes' were silenced.

I waited but disappointingly the public meeting failed to spark continuing local interest and I realised my efforts must continue.

So 85 year old Maisie Long, with chronic fatal emphysema, a four month patient of the top floor and a history hitherto of a packet of cigarettes a day, ran out of breath.

"Sister Connell found her dead during her rounds," Matron Jarvis explained. "The door was wide open and attracted her attention."

A mistake on my part. I'd been disturbed.

"The breathing apparatus –" began Reverend Lord.

"In place," confirmed the Matron. "Or rather back in place. The machine had not been turned off. She'd been smothered."

Again, thought Dr Patel, there was no evidence. Everything was normal. The dry leathery face, thinned by age and nicotine, looked peaceful. The liver-spotted hands lay gently composed on the sheet. The pillow carefully replaced behind the silver hair bore no marks, lipstick nor saliva of the victim, no distinguishing marks of the perpetrator, whom he suggested wore gloves. All normal, except Mrs Maisie Long was dead.

They were all obviously in a quiet panic. Silence around the table. What had been a vague suspicion perhaps not even that, just an uncomfortable feeling, was now confirmed as a killing.

As I said, it was a mistake. I'd planned to turn off the machine then turn it back on, but I'd been interrupted and had to finish off Maisie physically in case she recognised me. And the other one was still a problem, how much had they seen?

"Police?" asked Amy Bennett, so softly some might not have heard.

"Yes, I'll see to it," Robert Carroll said hesitantly.

"Do we have to rush?" asked the Matron. "Apart from us here, Sister Connell is the only one who knows the facts."

"What do you mean, Avril?"

"What I mean is we don't know enough yet.

Certainly Mrs Long is dead. Someone smothered her. But who did so? Another patient? A staff member? One of us perhaps?"

"Really Avril!" Shaun Wilson's protests were drowned out.

"Yes, ridiculous, I know, but do you also see the foolishness of calling in the police, Andrew?"

Matron Jarvis continued: "The police will interview everyone. *Everyone.* We won't be able to keep such a thorough investigation secret from the public and those earlier deaths, whether or not they're linked with Maisie Long's, will come out too. What reputation d'you think Twilight's nursing home will enjoy then?"

"The whole place will be shut down," cautioned Wilson in a show of unity. "Probably skeleton staff."

"And the other patients will find out and become frightened."

"But Avril, we can't do nothing!"

"Of course not, Robert, but I suggest we wait a while. The death could have been caused by another patient. One of the dementia's who got out or our local insomniac Lady Jane. It's the most likely explanation and it will come out. Someone will talk and we can quietly deal with the police with no public fuss."

"There are other patients here to be considered," the Chairman conceded.

"And who must be protected," said Reverend Lord.

"Then we must lift security," said Carroll in almost a grumble, "and night rates are expensive."

"But are we in agreement Matron's suggestion be agreed with?" said V.J. Patel with a touch of impatience.

"I think it's a sensible course for the moment, we can address increased costs later," Carroll agreed, recognising more important issues than a larger budget deficit, "but where do you stand Doctor and you, Marion, as our hospital visitor? The rest of us are answerable to the Village's main board, but you two are answerable to the government."

V.J. and Marion Turner looked across the table at each other and the woman shrugged her shoulders.

"If it's a patient I'd rather the matter be dealt with privately, both for the person and Twilight's reputation," Marion Turner said sensibly. "My role is to advise, perhaps correct, not damage."

"And I'm willing to take some time for much the same reasons as Ms Turner," said Dr Patel.

Which settled the main problem for the time being, I thought, but still left the observer, the one who might have seen me or something. The delay gave me time to find out who it was and to deal with them.

Life at Twilight resumed its routine but Dr Patel sensed an unease, not among the staff because to them the recent deaths were normal, but among the committee members.

Perhaps it was simply they all shared the secret of Maisie Long's death and were uncomfortable about this hidden truth. V.J. himself well understood the feeling. He had after all signed the death certificate in what some could claim were dubious circumstances, even if the cause of death had not technically been wrong.

He decided while he was prepared to wait as proposed by the Matron in the hope a patient would be revealed as the culprit, the agreement was not open ended. He could be seen as compromised if others decided to question his VMO position at the nursing home. Perhaps he could move things along in his own and Twilight's interest.

Visiting the nursing home was an almost daily occurrence and, importantly for his quest, at all hours of the day and night – a circumstance he recognised as also making him the possible offender.

Fortunately he always checked in through Casey, the night receptionist, but realised this was not a foolproof alibi. He resolved to be more careful and, if this did not prejudice patient care, limit his time in the building at night.

They were hardy souls in this rural area. Apart from broken bones from falls from farm machinery, road accidents and sick children, the Drummond regional hospital to which the government had accredited him did not test his skills. Complicated illnesses, trauma, difficult births or major accidents were swiftly dealt with by the Royal Flying Doctor Service – the Mantle of Safety for residents of the Australian bush. A circumstance which perfectly suited Dr V.J. Patel, giving him more time to observe his other responsibility.

Thus he became more aware, now noticing activities and behaviour he had previously ignored or overlooked. The nursing home had its secrets.

At night Todd spent a lot of time with his girlfriend. Granted there wasn't much for the young woman to do because visitors were few after hours and telephone calls even rarer, usually outgoing to his own mobile. Like others of the staff he did not live on site, his residence being at his primary occupation, the hospital.

What Todd did other than hang around Casey at night was a mystery. V.J. assumed she needed her sleep during the day but if Todd worked, he needed his sleep too.

The easy-going informality of the nursing home extended further, with Amy Bennett often accompanied on her visits by a big gangly teenage boy, who V.J. was told by Marion Turner was Amy's son.

"Paul, I think is his name. He's retarded and Amy brings him with her when her husband – they're separated – can't look after him. He's not dangerous, at least only to himself."

The doctor sometimes would see him wandering around the building alone when Amy was with a patient. The social worker did not visit at night, still …

And then there was Shaun Wilson and his attraction to a pretty Filipina nurse, who sometimes worked nights sorting laundry in a room off the ground floor. From the giggles they were not folding sheets or discussing union business.

He focused upon the nursing home committee members because he could not see other Twilight staff as culpable. He could not provide a motive for his community colleagues and it seemed much less likely that among those African and Asian nurses with traditional reputations of respect for the elderly and grateful for the job, there could be a murderer.

He wondered if others were taking a similar interest in each other as he was, conscious if they searched long and thoroughly enough nobody would be exempt from suspicion.

Not even Dr V.J. Patel.

His move over the mountains from the big city had not been orchestrated to escape its Mumbai-like size, but rather its knowledgeable Indian population and he had been remarkably lucky that there appeared no other countrymen living here.

Like Casey, like Amy Bennett, like Shaun, his secret was not a criminal offence, but it was of interest and would be of comment in the gossip of this smaller regional centre. Unlike the others, he was out of the ordinary.

I sensed an attitudinal change in my colleagues. Nothing specific, just a wariness among them as to who might be the perpetrator. There was no suggestion to my mind they thought anyone else in particular was responsible. We all had access.

I would have to be more careful, particularly as I haven't yet found out who might have seen me or seen something.

Dr Patel decided he needed a map of the nursing home, its entrances and exits, and found his little 'cupboard', as he called it, on the ground floor ideal as his work space. The enterprise grew, revealing more of the Twilight building than he had realised.

Each of the three floors accommodated twenty single rooms, ten on each side of a long central corridor, broken half-way by a lounge adjacent to the lifts. In keeping with the fire regulations there were continuing exit stairs at both ends of each floor, although V.J. thought they were more for show than effect: bed-ridden patients would have no chance of negotiating the steep descent. The stairs simply complied with the law.

Access to the lifts was opposite the reception desk on the ground floor, which in turn was adjacent to

Matron Jarvis' office, used at night by Sister Connell as her base.

The space for these administrative areas was taken from the ground floor nursing bedrooms. No space had been created for his own cupboard: it was tucked away under the stairs at the north end of the building, and as he had noted looked out across the road to the neglected neighbouring park.

The complex, Dr Patel observed from these closer observations, was compact. The doors both to outside and to inside were opened by keys held by all committee members and a few other staff. There was no nurse's station on each floor. Presumably Sister Connell's night patrols were considered adequate – or had been – for the security of the patients behind their unlocked doors.

Most of the residents on the two top floors were bedridden, something he knew but had not really considered as to why. The truth was they were not going anywhere but out. These higher floors were effectively a hospice.

V.J. would have liked to know if Sister Connell had a regular roster for her security night walks and more importantly, who else knew of it, but he was not confident to ask and decided he would have to resort to spying.

He realised this was an unreliable surveillance

method and expensive in terms of his own sleep, but the Sister's timing was important as she was the only officer on duty at these apparently dangerous overnight hours. Like most institutions meals provided from the main hospital kitchen were delivered early at five o'clock in the afternoon and breakfast after daybreak.

The ground floor accommodated more mobile patients whom he noted had not yet been visited by the smotherer. V.J. wondered if this was because the area was more public: Casey, maybe Todd, Sister Connell. Or if the very extra mobility of its elderly posed a problem for the killer.

Dr Patel continued his nursing home visits with a keener interest in his colleagues: Amy Bennett, Shaun Wilson, and Matron Jarvis, whom he saw more regularly than Marion Turner and Reverend Lord with their wider hospital responsibilities. Even Robert Carroll put in an occasional appearance, having a relative or friend accommodated in Twilight's nursing building.

None of which helped V.J. to identify the offender.

He developed a new sleep pattern. He ate early in the staff canteen, no matter of comment because he was not in the habit of having his meals with anyone else, then slept until midnight when he slipped across to the nursing home and into his cupboard via the exit stairs door with his key. There he sat quietly until he felt it safe to emerge into the sleeping upper floors accessed by the fire stairs.

He made no attempt to enter patient's rooms. In fact standing silently in the darkness below the illuminated green exit sign just inside the stair door gave him an uninterrupted view of the entire floor with its dim night lights.

He regretted the waste of electricity these illuminations caused and wished for his own reasons how much better it would have been if all corridor lights came on only when someone entered the area. Torches admittedly kept the brightness down but it seemed a little like Florence Nightingale's lamp for Sister Connell to be using this method and hardly secure.

The second night of his early morning vigil coincided with a fierce storm with rain and wind beating against the building. That night the doctor was on the top floor and waited in futile puzzlement for Sister Connell to visit. The following night he again positioned himself on the third floor, reasoning the Sister's security check might have been confined to some urgent weather crisis on the second floor the previous early morning. Again Sister Connell did not show up.

Perhaps she didn't conduct security checks at all, Dr Patel wondered? Maybe she only ventured up here when she had a murderous job to do?

Perhaps it explained why night security had not been increased. Sister Connell was raising objections and Robert Carroll's claimed breakdown of negotiations over staffing and costs with Shaun Wilson was untrue. Or maybe Carroll or the unionist had their own reasons for preventing extra overnight patrols – apart that is from the Chairman's mania with costs.

These thoughts worried V.J. as he hurried down the fire stairs to the ground floor.

Like everywhere else and except for the dim night lights the corridor was in darkness, save for the brighter area radiating from Casey's reception desk around the corner in the centre. The next door opening onto the corridor but separated he knew from Casey by a brick wall was Matron Jarvis' office, now identified by a strip of floor light.

As he watched the door opened and Matron slowly backed out, simultaneously locked in an intimate farewell embrace with whom the doctor thought from height and dress to be Sister Grace Connell.

V.J. had seen Todd occasionally in the nursing home corridors during his own visits to the building.

The young man always had been on the ground floor but the doctor was curious as to why he was present at all and during the day when Casey was off duty.

Nevertheless he was surprised when, before he could think up an acceptable excuse for asking him his business there, Todd hailed him one evening as he was walking toward the staff canteen for an early meal. Casey and Todd were heading in the same direction.

"What did you think of the death with dignity meeting?" the young man began without preamble.

Dr Patel replied in his quiet way that it was healthy to publicly discuss such contentious issues.

"And what d'you think about it?" probed Todd.

It was not an easy question for a medical practitioner

to answer, he explained carefully, but before he could elaborate the young man interrupted.

"How can you hold any position except for support if you are committed to relieving pain and suffering?"

At this point having reached the canteen Casey, a plump motherly girl, offered to order and collect the three meals, reminding Todd she had limited time before taking up her night receptionist duties.

"And we do relieve people of their physical and yes, mental, pain," said V.J. as Casey moved away, thankfully he thought.

"But not everybody," challenged Todd. "Our hospitals and nursing homes are full of people who are being deliberately kept alive when they'd rather be dead."

"I don't think there are that many," Dr Patel argued, thinking of those in Twilight happy to continue to live despite their more limited physical circumstances.

"Well lots," the young man conceded and resumed the attack: "Why aren't they given the choice?"

Dr Patel had no logical answer to this question so he remained silent. How do you explain the moral attitudes built up over centuries to someone who does not support them and indeed apparently cannot find a sensible reason for doing so?

"Why should other people insist we live when some want to die," Todd pressed on. "Why do we allow people to die in war but not otherwise?"

It's not the same, thought V.J., but it's too deep an argument to pursue in the canteen.

"Why do we keep people alive with pain killing drugs which often ultimately kill them? It's hypocritical!"

"It eases their pain," Dr Patel defended.

"For no purpose if they want to die," Todd argued. "Remember death with dignity is only for those who want it. It's not compulsory."

"There are moral as well as medical – "the doctor began.

"Only for some!" he was interrupted. "The churches particularly and the lily-livid politicians who are frightened of their imagined influence."

Casey returned with a tray of meals and an expression which suggested she had heard all this too often before.

Todd ignored his shepherd's pie to pursue what V.J. thought a dangerous argument.

"Our politicians are always banging on about costs. Do they realise how much they could save in expensive hospital and nursing home beds, palliative care too, if they let those who want to go, go?"

"Eat you dinner, Todd, before it gets cold," Casey said maternally.

"You can't put a price on life."

"Which is why most of us don't use the cost argument, because it strengthens our opposition's case that we're driven by financial not compassionate reasons. But if you put aside emotions, think how much money could be saved keeping alive those who don't want to live which could be used for those who do? Children, for example."

Dr Patel worried how such an approach to life and death could be controlled so, conscious his lasagne was growing cold and sticky, pointed out without defining them how the choices could be subject to abuse.

"The greedy relatives again," Todd said dismissively, "after grandma's money or house. That, along with palliative care being everyone's solution, is the defence of the indefensible. Look at overseas, Europe, USA, where they've managed to counter that argument. We could either borrow or create our own legal protections."

As they departed to Casey's night time job Dr Patel wondered how far Todd's commitment extended to the rightness and compassion of death with dignity.

With a few exceptions the more mobile patients in the nursing home were accommodated upon the ground floor, from where with their walking frames and occasional walking stick they could access Twilight's lawns and gardens.

The exceptions included Jane, Lady Grey, widow of a knighted local pastoralist who, perhaps inevitably, found her name reshuffled to England's tragic aspirant to the throne, beheaded in 1554.

She was scatty, tending to memory loss, but her principle problem for the staff was she was an insomniac, taken to wandering the home's corridors at night. She had never been known to enter anyone else's room but most people believed this was only a matter of time.

Unsurprisingly Lady Jane Grey had been considered as the smotherer, until it was realised she had neither the strength nor the knowledge to commit such a crime.

Nevertheless she remained a threat, at least to me, because from a comment she made during my visits I identified her as the person who saw me or something when Maisie Long died. Nothing definite mind, just a question she asked was I unable to sleep too and taken to night wanderings?

It was enough for me to postpone my normal activities to concentrate on Lady Jane and walking the corridors' early mornings until I found her.

For his part Dr Patel continued his own nocturnal activities: dining early, slipping into his cupboard under the stairs and patiently waiting, sometimes nodding off to sleep, until the dark morning hours.

When not dozing he had enough to think about. Todd's zealotry for death with dignity, Amy Bennett's strapping retarded son, the lesbian relationship of Matron Jarvis and Sister Connell – which might delay, prevent, night rounds – all muddied the waters without necessarily pointing to a killer.

And they were not the only suspects. All committee members had easy access at all hours to the nursing home. Why not Robert Carroll, Marion Turner, the dedicated unionist or Reverend Lord? People he knew little or nothing about? What about himself and his secret back in Mumbai?

It had rained earlier and a mist had settled outside, which may or may not have muffled the scream and something which bounced, bumped down the stairs above his hideout. As his window looked out onto the road and overgrown park opposite he could see nothing of the result of what appeared to be a fall.

Time went by, minutes, then he saw a shadowy indistinct figure disappearing away into the mist across the road and into the park.

What to do? He waited quietly but there was no clamour, no running feet or shouts. Just the silence of the grave, which he thought was indeed the situation.

Finally he thought it was safe to move and slipped out of his cupboard. Lady Jane Grey lay at the foot of the concrete fire stairs below the green exit sign. He knew she was dead but carefully using a handkerchief to feel the pulse, he confirmed.

Then he crossed to the exit and let himself out into the cool early morning air.

"A terrible accident," intoned the Reverend Lord. "I hope the poor woman didn't suffer and may the Lord have mercy upon her soul."

"Bound to happen, though," said Marion Turner. "She was well-known for wandering around at night."

Which seemed to be the committee's general consensus, V.J. noted, as they moved on to the funeral arrangements, having read the findings of a Coroner's Court following police advice of death by misadventure.

"Even though she had no known relatives, I doubt the chapel will suffice. She was so well known locally we must use St Paul's in town," decided Robert Carroll. "Ideally all the committee should attend."

And I'd be a fool not to, I reasoned. This was no time to be drawing attention to myself.

The doctor was not a lunch person. Years of crowded waiting rooms had seen him conserving his time, so he often took a short break by walking around the grounds. After the often oppressive atmosphere of the patients' rooms with their bottles, tablets, disinfectants and overall aged smell it was a relief to breath fresh air.

He walked from the nursing home's main entrance after the meeting broke up and the participants headed for the canteen. An idea encouraged him to walk out of the nursing home grounds and across the road to the overgrown park.

He remembered the shadowy indistinct figure from that night crossing toward the park. It had rained earlier and he recalled as he made his way back to his flat he had felt cold.

What if whoever it was had worn a coat which had brushed against trees or shrubs as they made their way through the wet, dripping bush?

He did not imagine the person had simply blundered away from the murder scene – Dr Patel was sure this was another killing even if there was a different method – but possibly the killer's regular escape route from the nursing home.

And almost opposite the exit door was a rough dirt trail into the park of a type created by walkers wanting to take a short cut somewhere.

It was dry underfoot now. Not that footprints would have been useful because the police were not yet involved and a lot of explaining would have been necessary to bring them in at this late stage.

Dr Patel moved slowly along the trail, carefully noting the bushes and lower hanging branches of the trees lining the uneven route.

Most had smooth leaves capable of taking nothing from a passing body but then the edge of a blackberry patch intruded, overlooked or ignored by rangers charged with eradicating the pest, and there it was, a few wisps of dark wool.

It was not conclusive the doctor reminded himself as he picked the items from the thorns and placed them in a handkerchief. They could belong to anyone's apparel, but he thought not too many people had used this short cut recently. The unpredictable rainy weather of late would dissuade most, even all except perhaps someone who had no choice?

But what could he do with this possible evidence, V.J. pondered, as he walked back to Twilight?

It could only be contributory, certainly not proof the wearer of whatever it was, was the killer. If indeed there was a killer, that Lady Jane Grey did not accidentally tumble down the stairs on her nocturnal walk. It was even only his conjecture the figure he saw retreating from view in the dark and mist to cross the road had come from the nursing home.

I don't do lunch. A sandwich satisfies me usually and today was no exception. Thus I saw Dr Patel from where I was standing and eating in the gardens going onto the dirt track opposite leading into the overgrown park. It was so unusual for my quiet methodical colleague I reacted uneasily. It was so out of character it had to have meaning and that meaning I was sure included me.

Pity, because otherwise the day held future promise. The irritant and possible threat Lady Jane Grey was dead and I could now get on with my purpose, which had perforce of her presence forced postponement until she had been taken care of. This presented a problem, because the delay had created a backlog which I could hardly deal with quickly. A massacre would only draw unfavourable attention.

I would have to be selective, choosing patients with care. Spreading them out would allow my arm to strengthen again, smothering even the elderly took effort and Lady Jane had fought for her balance. I would also have the chance to consider if and how I dealt with Dr Patel.

V.J.'s excursion to the wild park had a consequence he now foresaw and wondered why he hadn't considered before: where did the track lead?

One quiet afternoon when most of the patients were having their afternoon nap, snoring noisily with open mouths, he again crossed the road and climbed the trail through the undergrowth. He was surprised within fifteen minutes he was free of the tangled bushes and on the edge of the manicured sixth green of the local golf course.

The so-called park simply was a scrub barrier enclosing the fairways and to the right and the left a concrete path meandered across and around the neat eighteen holes. Beyond he could see streets and houses.

Sensibly he wondered who from the nursing home committee was a member of the golf club – not that it mattered much with activities at night – but perhaps importantly who lived in those distant streets.

Robert Carroll he knew from the telephone directory lived in a large comfortable house on a hill overlooking the regional centre, while Reverend Lord, a widower, had a flat on his churches' premises. Neither were in the direction of the rough trail but that hardly mattered: they could have parked their car nearby under cover of darkness or even walked.

Apart from Matron Jarvis, who had a flat in the grounds of the main hospital, and V.J. himself who was similarly accommodated nearby, everyone lived off site.

Privacy limitations made his investigations difficult and on the pretext of keeping in touch should a medical emergency arise he obtained an address on the other side of town for Amy Bennett and a flat across the road for Casey and Todd.

Shaun Wilson looked promising because he lived a couple of streets away from the golf club. However the union representative's prospects diminished when, following up his telephone number in his small sedan, Dr Patel encountered a pregnant woman escorting two children to a car in the driveway of a weatherboard house. It seemed unlikely the man could slip away from his family in the early hours of the morning, although the giggling in the laundry room might be explained.

The doctor could find no addresses for Grace Connell, the night sister and Matron's girlfriend, nor Marion Turner. Connell wore a thin wedding ring so it was possible she was using her maiden name for her nursing work and Marion Turner had a mobile, so didn't need to be in the telephone directory. Not being a permanent employee the hospital visitor probably had another job, but V.J. couldn't see much point in following that course.

He would have to wait until opportunities arose and further evidence came forward to identify these two addresses.

Nevertheless he found it difficult to identify any of these people as killers. And while he had not factored in Todd as a genuine suspect since he noticed him about during the day, the mystery of his nursing home attendance was explained by a ground floor patient the doctor was examining.

"If you see Todd ask him to see me", the elderly woman croaked as Dr Patel packed his stethoscope.

"Something you need, Mrs Lewis?"

"Yes, I want to place a bet at the TAB," she said hoarsely.

Todd, it transpired, was the home's runner to the centre's betting shop, earning his income from racing tips Twilight's knowledgeable patients' gave him.

"**S**mothered?"

"How else? She wasn't on a breathing apparatus," Matron Jarvis declared.

"I only saw her yesterday," Marion Turner said, inconsequently thought V.J. Patel.

"Surely it's time for the police?" asked Reverend Lord.

"Why, Andrew?" asked Robert Carroll. "We have no evidence Mrs Gordon was murdered. We only suspect so. Like most of the others she just stopped breathing."

"And do we tell the police about the others?"

"Difficult not to," said Marion Turner, indirectly taking sides with the Chairman. "Otherwise why single out Mrs Gordon alone for investigation?"

"Marion's right," agreed Matron Jarvis. "We can't bring in the police now with our suspicions without explaining why we didn't do so before and particularly with Maisie Long."

"We might not have any choice," V.J. said quietly.

"Why is that, Doctor? The family?"

"The family," Dr Patel confirmed.

Matron Jarvis had reported old Mrs Gordon's family had expressed shock and disbelief at her passing.

"Old, bedridden, incontinent," said her son, Bruce, "but she didn't look like dying."

As Matron Jarvis told the committee she sensed a rising anger in his tone.

"It simply could be old age."

"Of course, Reverend Lord, but it will still take some inquiries to establish that, even without involving the police, and if there are any doubts the police will come in. Otherwise … "

"Otherwise what, Doctor? "

"Our neglect, Ms Turner."

"That's absurd," exclaimed Robert Carroll. "Our patients are well cared for. The family wouldn't have a leg to stand on."

"They can still try. A law case, publicity, costs. No matter who wins we don't come out looking too good."

"We certainly don't want that!" said Robert Carroll, alert to the money consequences. "Any suggestions?"

"The police," said V.J. firmly.

In the silence which followed the Doctor explained.

"Our doubts were raised by Mrs Long's death because of its circumstances, the breathing apparatus being removed. This was comparatively recent, so do we need to mention the earlier deaths? Now Mrs Gordon has raised further concerns. We can be seen to be acting responsibly."

"And Lady Jane Grey?"

"There's nothing to suggest foul play, Matron," despite my own reservations, he thought. "We don't have to mention what Reverend Lord referred to as a terrible accident."

"Well, if you think it's the lesser of the two evils," the Chairman agreed reluctantly. "You've signed all the death certificates, Dr Patel."

"It would not be the first time a doctor has made a misdiagnosis and these circumstance, if they do involve a crime, would be extraordinary. Beyond most medical practitioner's experience."

This development I had not foreseen and it threw my plans into disorder. How would the police approach the investigation, would my relatively easy access to the rooms be challenged by heightened security? Whatever, it overrode any plans I had to deal with the nosy doctor.

" … I'll get in touch," Robert Carroll was concluding, "and you should all hold yourselves in readiness to be interviewed. Meantime not a word outside these walls. The media will be onto it – and us – soon enough."

As he made his way back to the main hospital block Dr Patel wondered if bringing in the police would change anyone's behaviour, particularly the innocent, which could complicate matters.

obert Carroll contacted the local police who sent a sergeant to Twilight. He looked around the building, took notes and departed. This was well outside the Friday night pub patrols and traffic accidents and two plain clothes officers turned up several days later from the region's central headquarters and began interviewing the committee members.

At the Chairman's suggestion they used the main hospital's board room, a discrete place away from the nursing home itself which thus held less chance of curious interest from visitors and staff. They inspected the building itself and its rooms after hours.

The discretion employed kept the local media from learning the purpose of the police visit. Nursing home deaths were for the obituary columns anyway and the funeral of such a prominent older citizen as Jane, Lady Grey already had been reported without the circumstances of her death being questioned.

Fitting in the interviews with the busy schedule of committee members and Sister Connell and Casey took time and V.J. Patel was among the last.

"You say Mrs Maisie Long's death was the first and looked suspicious. Why wasn't it reported immediately?" Detective Sergeant Rafferty asked at one point. His colleague Griffin was writing the notes. Both had taken off their coats and loosened their ties for the day was warm and the room not air-conditioned. They looked ready to get physical but Dr Patel knew from experience this was more Hollywood/Bollywood than reality.

"We thought it might be a disturbed patient," he said carefully.

"You allow your patients to wander at large?"

"No, our dementia ward is very secure. This lady we suspected was an insomniac taken to walking around at night. Like a lot of elderly people she was a little vague but otherwise healthy."

"So what was she doing in a nursing home?"

"There was nowhere else for her to go. No relatives and she couldn't really look after herself." And she could afford it, he thought.

"Where is she now?"

"She died. An accident." Dr Patel was sure the others had been asked these questions and hoped he was keeping to the accepted line. It was foolish to imagine they could avoid mention of Lady Jane Grey's death.

And predictably Rafferty asked: "How?"

"She fell down some fire stairs."

The doctor explained the death had been reported and because it was obviously an accident no further action had been taken.

"So why wasn't Mrs Maisie Long's death – which obviously was not an accident – reported?"

"Well it was officer, but not in the way people usually expect. These accidents happen from time to time in hospitals and nursing homes. If the culprit is also a patient laying charges can be difficult due to age and mental health."

"It's easier to claim natural causes?"

"It is, unless there is a complaint. Usually family."

"And does that happen a lot?"

"No."

Most family members and this included Maisie Long's, were shocked to see their loved one on a breathing apparatus struggling to stay alive, the face and the body deteriorated. Death was a relief, they decided.

"Why aren't the doors to the individual rooms locked at night?" asked Griffin looking up from his notes.

"It's safety over security," Dr Patel explained. "They can be checked on by the night sister."

If she gets around to it, he thought, remembering the scene at Matron Jarvis' door. Most are bedridden anyway, they're not going anywhere.

Dr Patel left the interview reassured he hadn't done too badly. He'd stuck to the generally agreed story and while having to bring in Lady Jane Grey's death had been unexpected, he couldn't see how he would have answered any differently from all the others without revealing what else he alone knew.

Which was the problem, because now the police were involved and he had given his version of events he had not given them the full story of his suspicions. What he had seen through the mist and found on the blackberry bush, Todd's outburst and Amy's son, Sister Connell's dilatory night rounds and the all-important reason he was hiding in his cupboard until the early hours of the morning in the hope of catching a killer.

How could retracting what he had said and telling them now what else he knew look convincing?

I believed I acquitted myself well. It was important to keep to a similar story, ideally the same story, as the others and it had not been possible to keep Lady Jane Grey's death out of it if she was to be considered for Maisie's death.

The two policemen, overweight from too many takeaways and casually dressed in sports clothes, gave me the impression the whole business was turning out to be no big deal. Nursing homes were where people died, how it happened might sometimes be a bit shady but hardly enough to turn it into a full blown investigation. Not with all the terrible things going on outside needing attention.

The police took their interview notes and themselves back to the region's central headquarters and the committee members resumed their daily routines.

Detective Sergeant Rafferty, who appeared to be the senior of the two, made it clear to Robert Carroll that the police were not happy with Twilight's security arrangements about either entrance to the rooms or to the building itself.

Carroll explained to the committee he had defended the decisions.

"He asked why our night sister couldn't look into every room if the doors couldn't be locked."

Grace Connell silently rolled her eyes but it was Matron Jarvis who answered for her.

"What purpose would that serve if it happened after her visit?"

"Exactly my point and I explained why the outside doors can't be secure with so many people holding keys."

Dr Patel silently agreed with him, if not for the arguments the Chairman put forward: any increased security would not protect patients from a killer inside the building.

Fortunately for the nursing home and the everlasting relief of the Chairman, when the police presence after the event was tipped off to the media it was diverted to the death fall of Lady Jane Grey as the reason for their visit to Twilight.

The widow of such a prominent local pastoralist and knight of the realm naturally would attract attention when she died in such tragic circumstances, Rolly Brown, chair of the hospital's main board, told the media after being briefed by Robert Carroll. It was normal, indeed prudent, to conduct an investigation and as a responsible organisation this is what they had done.

Then Helena Lawrence was smothered.

This ninety four year old woman had lain crippled from a horse riding accident years before, which initially saw her confined to a wheel chair. Now blind and incontinent she was bedridden, visited regularly by her devout Catholic daughter, Carmen.

"She just stopped breathing?" the woman asked incredulously through tears across the desk from Matron Jarvis.

"She was very old, Mrs Kelly, and not in the best of health – "

"I know that, I visited her every day!" Her husband, Patrick, stood silently beside her. "Why didn't you do something?"

"It's not that simple. Resuscitation often isn't successful."

"I want an autopsy," demanded Carmen Kelly.

"She was upset, of course," the Matron told the committee meeting convened for this latest crisis. "And critical of our procedures."

"Will she cause trouble, d'you think?" asked Robert Carroll.

"Hard to say, Robert. Mrs Kelly believes life is precious, as we all do, and that people should be kept alive at all costs, irrespective of their condition or circumstances. She doesn't think we do enough to uphold that basic belief."

It's a question of choice, Dr Patel decided, remembering Todd's conversation in the canteen and wondered if it was right for others to make the choice for someone else to live or die.

"We can't ignore these deaths anymore," Reverend Lord interjected. "It's three at least now. We'll have to bring the police back."

"What evidence do we have, Andrew?" asked Marion Turner. "Suspicions yes, but nothing definite."

"And why haven't we raised our doubts before with the police?" Robert Carroll worried aloud, confirming to V.J. that everyone had held to the same story. "It will be awkward going back on our words. It will look like a conspiracy to cover up the truth."

"Nobody will look good," Matron Jarvis confirmed.

"So we do nothing?" asked Reverend Lord.

"It might be wiser to do nothing for the time being," Amy Bennett said sensibly. "Mrs Kelly is very upset at her mother's death but she will heal. I'll talk to her."

Spoken like a caring social worker, thought Dr Patel, but there was wisdom in the suggestion, especially with two other deaths involved. How to explain those and perhaps reopen the fall of Lady Jane Grey?

They were now all stuck in a web of lies which benefited nobody except the killer. The only way to resolve the dilemma was to catch or expose the culprit. Dr Patel would have to resume his nocturnal snooping or maybe take a more dramatic step to achieve the aim.

Lucia Genova's death brought even more trouble to Twilight than that of Helena Lawrence.

A member of a large and volatile Italian family, the uproar became public with her sons' demanding to know what was happening at the nursing home where people stopped breathing. Their association with Carmen Kelly's family through their Catholic church added verisimilitude to the claim.

It also saw the return of Rafferty and Griffin with unpleasant news.

"Another two deaths reported by your local police seemed like Oscar Wilde's comment about losing parents, Doctor," said Rafferty, displaying a literary knowledge which surprised V.J., "so we decided to check back upon your committee members' antecedents. Routine, you understand."

"Interestingly we haven't found much," he continued.

"Privacy?" Dr Patel said hopefully.

"That depends. Mr Carroll and the Reverend Lord had records from their military and religious backgrounds, Mrs Bennett is a long-term local and there's Matron Jarvis …"

Here the policeman stopped, whatever they had found out was nobody else's business. "The others, all from elsewhere, have proved more difficult. Interstate report two or three possibly similar cases – old people smothered – but it's impossible to prove a deliberate act was committed and no genuine suspects anyway. Certainly nothing like the events here."

Rafferty paused, but Patel knew what was coming, why he had been personally summoned to the temporary police operations room: he had not yet been mentioned.

"And then there's you, Doctor."

"Bombay, well Mumbai now," the detective sergeant continued to Dr Patel's uncomfortable silence. "And a death."

"A young woman, I understand, and a botched abortion."

"Yes, "said Dr Patel quietly. "But I was not responsible."

"For the death or the pregnancy?"

"The former. Look officer," stupidly he couldn't decide how to address the policeman, "in India we have a caste system which in certain primitive areas is inflexible. I grew up in such a place and met – well, fell in love – with a girl who was above my station."

"But you're a doctor."

"And with a degree from England but it makes no difference. I wasn't from the lowest of the low, the untouchables or Dalits, but I wasn't of her rank. Irrespective of my achievements rising from comparative poverty, I couldn't – "

"And?" Rafferty, and Griffin for that matter, now appeared the uncomfortable.

"She fell pregnant." What a banal word for the accidental result of the ecstasy of sex. He still couldn't mention her name after all this time.

"We fled to Mumbai but her family followed. Anxious to absolve their shame."

"Mumbai is a huge city where you think you could hide, but it's not so simple. We were found and she was spirited away – kidnapped you would say – and forced to have an abortion."

"And she died."

"Yes. It was best for her family, she was no longer a virgin, damaged goods and the result of impregnation by a man of a lower caste, even a doctor. I've often wondered how efficiently the operation was carried out."

"That's murder," exclaimed Griffin, obviously not well versed in the ways of the world. "Couldn't you have gone to the police?"

"No. Evidence would be needed and prejudices run deep, even in the police force. Besides the Indian justice system, even though inherited from the British, is such a tangled mess I would have been an old man by the time anything came to Court far less judgement."

"So you came to Australia."

"Yes. Rumours suggested that her family's honour could be further satisfied if I was charged with the abortion, quite possible with enough money. So it was dangerous to stay but I was disgusted too with my country and its inequality and attitudes. My British qualifications got me here but I realised I couldn't escape my past in a large city. We Indian professionals mix together, so I moved here."

"Thank you for that background, Dr Patel. I'm sorry if you found it distressing, however it's important we know those details." Rafferty said, although V.J. noted the policeman did not indicate he was satisfied he was no longer a suspect. He wondered what they had found out about the other committee members.

Again I thought I'd done alright and the police hadn't been able to track me back and tie me to Mum's death. Leastways they didn't call me in for a grilling like the doctor apparently.

The inquiry into Lucia Genova's death intensified, the police thorough in their investigations into people's whereabouts.

While there was no suggestion the police diligence was encouraged by the Genova's public campaign for a detailed examination – even a royal commission was suggested – the family's persistence was unsettling and nobody wanted to be accused of treating the old lady's death casually.

She perhaps had died earlier than the others and whether or not this was a change from the killer's normal early morning behaviour, it opened up the suspect list. There were plenty to choose from.

That evening Amy Bennett's son had turned up distressed at Casey's reception desk and eventually made her to understand he could not find his mother. She had mislaid her handbag somewhere visiting patients, she later told them. Todd went off to find her leaving

Paul with Casey. Both the searcher and the searched for were away long enough to smother a bedridden person like Lucia Genova.

Reverend Lord also was in the building giving communion to another aged resident and Sister Connell was on her regular rounds, or so she said.

Even Dr Patel was on the ground floor assessing the condition of a ninety three year old's extravagantly unnecessary hip operation

These activities all were revealed when they met at the reception desk before going home. An accidental build-up because the police were waiting there to establish people's movements. The exercise provided an alibi for nobody, even those who were not present.

V.J. in the later silence of his cupboard realised he would need to change his tactics. Creeping around in the early morning darkness on the off chance of inter-cepting the killer was too hit or miss and dangerous as well, as Lady Jane Grey had found to her cost.

He waited until the next committee meeting, when following now commonplace grumbles about the continuing police presence and the Genova's also continuing public complaints about Twilight's lack of patient care, Dr Patel raised the subject of vacant beds.

"On my reckoning we have five," he explained. "Do we have a waitlist? These facilities are expensive."

Reverend Lord thought it premature to be filling vacancies now with Lucia Genova buried only recently, but he was overruled by the ever cost conscious Chairman.

"We should go to our waitlist," Robert Carroll decided. "Discretely of course – private phone calls inviting inspection."

"Only two people have been publicly identified as dying here," Matron Jarvis contributed. "It's hardly excessive for a nursing home of sixty patients."

"We do have a waiting list," pointed out Shaun Wilson reasonably, probably worried about staff employment.

"Might it be difficult with the Genova's public campaign against Twilight?" asked the Matron.

Reverend Lord reconsidered. "Perhaps we shouldn't deny those in need the comfort of Twilight," he suggested. "I'll have a word with Father Murphy at St Mary's," he offered, "and ask him to intercede with the Genova's."

When this somewhat generous comment was greeted with silence around the table, Dr Patel added slyly: "We might have a sixth vacancy."

"What d'you mean, Doctor?" Matron Jarvis asked accusingly.

"Nothing sinister, Matron," V.J. replied depreciatingly. "Mrs Agnes Cummins seems not long for us from my examinations and her wishes. She's very uncomfortable."

"Room 307?"

"Yes." This was working better than he had hoped.

Dr Patel had wondered the motive for these recent killings and reached the tentative conclusion they were elderly bedridden people who probably had not long to live. Their quality of life was poor: incontinent, lacking sensory abilities, fed with drips or, in Mrs Long's case, reliant on a breathing apparatus. They had no future and someone had taken it upon themselves to help them die with what little dignity remained to them.

nstead of silently wandering the corridors of Twilight's second and third floors, Dr Patel concentrated upon the area around Room 307 and Mrs Agnes Cummins.

He could not have explained why he did so, least of all to the entrenched police, except that he had publicised the name of somebody who was vulnerable and thus needed to be protected, depending upon your life or death views.

Fortunately Mrs Cummins' room was only fourth from the exit stairs and by keeping that door slightly ajar he could see the whole dimly lit corridor and Sister Connell's occasional but regularly timed security patrol.

By the third early morning the Doctor began to wonder if his trap had worked. Leaning against the heavy door in the darkness, the cold from the concrete floor of the stairwell penetrating his shoes …

Then below he heard the sounds of someone else on the stairs and realised too late he had trapped himself. How else was the killer to reach patients' rooms without the risk of being seen?

V.J. quickly slipped through the exit door and hurried to Agnes Cummins' room where he hid behind her door. He heard the heavy door to the stairwell click shut, alerting whoever was coming up.

Dr Patel was surprised when he heard the exit door reopen, imagining he had scared off the climber. Instead soft footsteps came along the corridor, paused, and a pencil thin light picked up Agnes Cummins' false teeth in water on the bedside table and then her aged face as the shadowy figure moved into the room and toward the bed.

Here it paused and the free hand checked the old woman's breathing before Reverend Lord put out the light and moved out of Room 307.

The doctor waited for what he thought was a decent interval, listening for the closing of the exit door, then stepped into the now empty corridor. He realised he could not follow Andrew Lord down the fire stairs nearby without being seen or heard.

He would have to traverse the entire corridor to the other northern exit fire stairs and perhaps risk meeting Sister Connell.

Dr Patel set off as quickly as he quietly could, past the lounge and locked lifts, and the widely ajar door of Room 311. Instinct checked his pace: the doors were unlocked but not open.

The blow – it was more of a shove – he received as he unwisely poked his head inside Room 311 knocked him back into the door frame, compounding the damage to his skull. He was slipping to the floor when the figure barrelled over him and V.J. desperately grabbed at the coat for balance before lapsing into unconsciousness.

He was not found until the morning shift and Agnes Cummins was dead – smothered.

I meant our doctor no harm but I risked exposure when he turned down the corridor and decided to become curious about my hiding place, where I had stupidly failed to close off the door. Fortunately he still had a pulse, so I could drag him into Room 311 behind the door and safely leave him and continue with my work.

"So what were you doing in the nursing home in the early hours of this morning?" Detective Sergeant Rafferty asked.

Dr Patel was propped up in a main hospital private room bed with a throbbing headache and a bandaged skull. Hitting the door frame had done the most injury, the shove to his face was mild in comparison.

V.J. guessed it was a betrayal of sorts of his committee colleagues but he could not see any other way out but to tell the truth: the mounting deaths, including Lady Jane Grey, his suspicion there was a killer among the members of the committee and his amateurish attempts to find this perpetrator.

He did not mention Matron Jarvis and Sister Connell, nor Amy Bennett's retarded son Paul nor Casey's boyfriend Todd and the freedom enjoyed by everyone to visit at all hours.

Even Reverend Lord's own nocturnal visit went unmentioned, now seen as a kindly if foolish attempt to see if Mrs Cummins was safe, although it was a mystery why the churchman had left his check up for several nights.

He realised, despite the pain of achieving it, that his position in the eyes of the police had improved. People who were attacked and left unconscious in a hospital room are hardly likely to be the culprit's for a murder nearby.

"And you've no idea who hit you?" Rafferty asked when he had finished.

"None at all," the Doctor replied. "Although it was more like a shove. Not powerful, so I think it might be a woman."

"Or a weak man," the policeman ruminated. "Anyway, it won't happen again. We've posted constables in the corridors during the night hours until we've tracked down whoever it is."

"You say you grabbed their coat as you were falling to the floor," Rafferty continued. "We found some fibres in your hand. Not much but they're being analysed. We won't know for a while, they had to go to the big city lab, but I reckon they're wool and I thought maybe a scarf."

"And maybe I can help you a little further," Dr Patel replied.

Which was not the situation facing Robert Carroll at the next urgent committee meeting two days later.

Commiserations to Dr Patel, the bandage now removed, were perfunctory before the Chairman addressed the headlines on the newspaper before him.

"We tried Robert," Reverend Lord said resignedly.

"They don't know the full story, just a few deaths, but this is bad enough," Robert agreed, but not really mollified.

Mysterious deaths at Twilight said the leading story, then listed Helena Lawrence, Lucia Genova and Agnes Cummins. Lady Jane Grey and earlier deaths were not mentioned, leading Dr Patel to suspect the story had been fuelled by Carmen Kelly and the Genova family.

"It's only speculation at present," said Carroll. "Talk of a virus or food poisoning, they haven't gotten around to murder yet."

"But in some ways this is worse," Matron Jarvis exclaimed. "Our reputation's at stake. Once these rumours start circulating people will be querying our standards, our quality control, then the Health Department will step in."

"We have nothing to fear about health standards, Avril," protested an alarmed Robert Carroll.

"Of course not, but mud sticks. It would almost

be better if people knew they were being deliberately removed."

Perhaps, I thought, and an anonymous note to the newspaper would fix it. But I couldn't see how it would help my cause. People needed to be shown why what was happening.

"Only a matter of time then, now the police are about," someone murmured, possibly Marion Turner.

"Why?" asked Dr Patel.

"So our nursing home's good reputation isn't being trashed by lies," Matron Jarvis said scornfully, as if the reason was obvious.

"No, why are these patients in particular being killed," V.J. continued patiently.

"Random selection?" suggested Amy Bennett.

"Perhaps, but do they have something in common maybe?"

"Women?"

"A misogynist? I don't think so, principally because statistically there are more widows than widowers, more single women than single men, in nursing homes, so we shouldn't be misled by false premises."

"Religion?" offered Reverend Lord.

You of all people should know, thought Dr Patel, but he replied to his limited knowledge there were believers and non-believers, or at least given the ages, those of different faiths.

"Most of us saw most of these women from time to time. Can we identify a common thread which linked them?"

It was Marion Turner, the hospital visitor and probably the least likely to know, who nailed it.

"I wouldn't have seen them all, nor as regularly as most of you, my role here is not as personal," she said depreciatingly, "but thinking about those few I did see, they all wanted to die."

"So you say there's a fair chance we're dealing with someone whose motive is mercy killing?" Detective Sergeant Rafferty asked.

He was in belt and colourful braces today, coat off for the weather again was hot. Dr Patel stayed with suit and tie, his continuing lack of confidence keeping him buttoned up, neat, tidy, and respectable.

"I think so," he replied cautiously. "There was unanimous agreement around the table the deceased women" and a few you don't know of, detective, he thought, "had all said at one time or another and to several of the committee, they had had enough. They wanted to die."

He remembered his conversation with Todd and the croaking wishes pleading for death he himself had heard on an almost daily basis from aging wrecks, whose shrivelled smelly bodies and broken down senses were felt by themselves to be an affront to humanity.

"Extreme isn't it, going around killing the elderly?"

"Is it? These are people whose usefulness is finished. Whatever their achievements in life it's over, they're confined permanently to a nursing home bed, often lonely, in discomfort and yes, pain. Is it any wonder some of them at least want to end their life now? There's no dignity left for them."

He almost could smell the antiseptic, the stale urine, the decay.

"So death with dignity, eh? Still extreme though."

The policeman was looking at him with renewed interest and V.J. realised his remarks could be misinterpreted, his credit with Rafferty gone. Time to backtrack.

"Death with dignity, mercy killing, voluntary assisted dying, euthanasia, might have different names or phrases but they're all addressing the same issue, which is gaining traction around the world," he explained. "It doesn't have to be compulsory as its opponents fear, but people are asking what compassion is there in keeping someone alive who doesn't want to be? Someone in pain, perhaps agony? It's elder abuse."

"So their opponents are no better than they are?"

"That's the argument." But don't get me started upon those who want to keep people alive as God's punishment for earlier sins in life.

"It's really a matter of choice, or should be if the politicians weren't so frightened of the moralists and churches. They should have a national referendum on the subject," he concluded.

"Meantime, we can't allow someone to go around killing people," Rafferty said.

"No, "agreed Dr Patel. "Even if they've lost patience with the law changing."

Or was it love, he wondered?

He considered the conversation later and was surprised his own feelings had altered, not to conviction but to confusion.

Dr Patel was no longer committed to life at all costs, to playing God and seeking relatively short-term procedures for keeping the elderly alive when they wanted to die. This new attitude went against all he had been taught and believed but the worthy aims of combatting pain and suffering were no longer clear cut.

Other considerations had been raised by the prominent national advocate and the earnest Todd. In a world where so much effort was directed against discrimination and upholding human rights why was something as fundamental as the right to die being ignored?

Habit held him to the old beliefs but he was uneasy.

"Any news on the wool pieces?"

V.J. had taken to visiting the office at the hospital when he saw the unmarked police sedan in the carpark. He believed the officers owed him some attention for providing the blackberry scraps, as he called them.

Rafferty clearly agreed because he was welcomed.

"They match," he confirmed. "Woollen scarf perhaps. Now we need to find the owner."

Which might not be easy, Dr Patel conceded. Whoever it was worked only at night when it was cold on these open slopes and plains which encompassed Drummond. During the day, certainly at this time of year, it was warm enough to work without a coat.

How to flush out the scarf wearer would not be simple and would require taking others into his confidence. A risky business when you didn't even know the sex of the offender.

Dr Patel however realised the field could be narrowed if he was willing to take a chance. He was influenced in his decision by two happenings which suggested the offender was a woman: the blow he received at Room 311 was more of a shove not a punch and secondly the visit of Reverend Lord to Agnes Cummins immediately prior to the incident probably ruled him out as the killer.

Which left Robert Carroll and Shaun Wilson as the only other male suspects. The law of averages seemed against the two men and anyway, Dr Patel had no choice.

"I can't see why you insist upon an evening meeting," Carroll said doubtfully, "when you won't give me a plausible reason."

"Please trust me, Mr Chairman," he pleaded. V.J. was reluctant to explain his plan in fear something might be leaked to the killer by accident.

"Our patients are safe at present with police in the corridors at night, but eventually the officers will be withdrawn and they will be vulnerable again," he continued in his soft voice. "What I propose is unorthodox but short of a spontaneous confession I can't see us finding the culprit otherwise."

"But you won't tell me why?" grumbled Carroll.

I can't, thought V.J., because it might not work.

"No. The evening meeting is only the beginning, there's more to what I have in mind."

"And if it doesn't work?"

"Then no harm is done. If the meeting doesn't work out as planned, I won't proceed further. I promise."

"It's not our usual practice," worried Carroll. "I suppose all members could make this extraordinary – yes, that's what we could call it. What d'you think, Andrew?"

Like Dr Patel, the Chairman had forgotten his male colleague while he wrestled with the unusual request. Now, decision made thought V.J., Carroll sought support.

"Unusual, Robert, even unprecedented, but if it helps keep our patients' safe from the evil surrounding them we have no choice. God works in mysterious ways ... "

"I'll set up a meeting as soon as I can," the Chairman said hurriedly, perhaps anticipating a homily.

Dr Patel advised the sceptical police.

"I hope you know what you're doing, Doctor," Rafferty said doubtfully. "It's unorthodox, but – "

"There's no risk," promised V.J. "All you have to do is be present."

"I was about to say we'll give it a try," Rafferty continued, with a nod to Griffin. "It might work."

It was odd to have an evening meeting but with our chairman going away as he explained and unclear when he would be back and the police in the corridors stopping me, it made no difference day or night to me. I realised I would have to attend, any absence would look suspicious at this fraught time. Just lie low, the police would not be here forever.

t was eight o'clock in the evening, already dark, and the committee all present were sitting around the table. At V.J.'s urging Sister Connell and Casey sat against the opposite wall facing him. As anticipated the night outside was chilly, the men wore sweaters, the women coats and scarves.

Robert Carroll opened the meeting in the formal way then seemed at a loss how to continue. He looked with desperate appeal to Dr Patel, sitting halfway along to his right.

"Thank you, Mr Chairman, I can take the agenda from here," the Doctor said. Opposite sat the woman with the woollen scarf around her neck.

"We have experienced a number of tragic deaths among our elderly residents, "Dr Patel began, looking around the table, "which initially we assumed to be from natural causes, until circumstances forced us to face an unpalatable truth these old people were being murdered."

"Hence the police," Matron Jarvis said impatiently. Did she have a later rendezvous, he wondered.

"Indeed, Matron, and it was then thought the deaths were a random selection. Only later in exchanges among ourselves did we find a common link."

The attention in the room now was undivided.

"All the dead had expressed a wish to die."

"Still supposition."

"Yes, it is, Ms Turner, even though, as I recall, you first suggested it might be the motive."

"So we have someone here who believes in and practices mercy killing?" asked Reverend Lord, obviously uncomfortable with the presence, the knowledge or both.

"We do and I have a good idea who it is."

Dr Patel explained about his cupboard bolthole and how he had used it as a hideout after Maisie Long's death to have early morning access to the upper floors of the nursing home. He deliberately did not mention what he had seen nor the secrets and suspicions he knew or harboured of his fellow committee members.

"So you could be the killer," called Sister Connell from the other side of the room.

"Except for some evidence," he defended, over

Chairman Carroll's angry rebuke at the audience interjection.

V.J. told them on the night Lady Jane Grey fell down the stairs to her death he had noticed a shadowy figure crossing the road to the wilderness park opposite the nursing home. Later, retracing those steps, he had found some wool fibres on a blackberry bush beside the trail through the park. These he had kept.

"The night Agnes Cummins' died, I was attacked near her room," the doctor continued. Only a sharp exclamation from Shaun Wilson betrayed most present had not known the full details.

"The police retrieved some wool fibres from my fingers when I fought with my assailant to retain my balance. The police confirm both sets are a match."

"They all wanted to die!" The statement was emphatically defiant.

"It's still murder," said Reverend Lord.

"Only in your medieval interpretation. Mercy killing goes on all the time. People kill their loved ones, spouses, relatives, to spare them further often agonising pain. Death with dignity simply extends this compassion to a wider population."

"It's illegal," Dr Patel contributed.

"At the moment. D'you know studies have shown over eighty percent of people in Australia are in favour of mercy killing? If our faint-hearted politicians would allow a referendum instead of being frightened of the churches, we'd romp it in."

Dr Patel knew this to be true. Even if some voters changed their mind, the margin would be enough for victory.

"There's no pain involved and the law could prevent abuses."

"No need to smother then? And you used gloves?" Suddenly curious.

"Of course. A simple injection. Keeping people alive when they don't want to live is age discrimination or elder abuse."

Back and forth across the room went the conversation while the rest of the committee watched with their eyes a deadly table tennis game.

"How can you be sure?"

"That they want to die? It can be established legally as is done overseas. Checks and balances built in, if you won't accept words from their own mouths."

"Official requests which overcome the argument that voluntary assisted dying –" V.J. was impressed at the careful choice of words so specific in avoiding an accidental death – "could be misused against young people. The thin edge of the wedge as opponents' claim."

"And yes," the voice continued, arguing the case

in a calm and unemotional tone, "I've heard the fear mongers' arguments about killing off old people by family or friends for their money or property, but has anybody considered this might be a sacrifice the old person wants to make? Shouldn't they have a say in whether or not they live or die and why? It's not compulsory."

"Nobody should play God," reproved Reverend Lord.

"I fully agree. But why should you, Reverend Lord, or you, Doctor Patel, decide someone should live when they don't want to do so? Aren't you playing God?"

"The Lord gives us life."

"And can take it away. But I suggest you are putting religion, a man-made theological construct, between God and a human being. Not everyone wants that, not even believers. Why should they be denied their choice because of the teachings of human middlemen?"

"Have you no sense of guilt?"

Reverend Lord was sounding more and more like an Old Testament prophet.

"None. No sorrow either. If we had sensible compassionate laws I would not have to practice death with dignity. These women wanted to die and I helped them, that's all. Nobody else would do anything. None of you, for example," there was rising anger in the voice,

"Checking out that all our bedridden wasted patients were as physically comfortable as possible with pre-scriptions from you, Doctor, and prayers from you, Reverend, while ignoring their pleas to die. I believe our justice system will judge me favourably because if society wouldn't do it, somebody had to lead the way."

And perhaps bring this contentious matter to a head in the public arena, thought Dr Patel. A sacrificial lamb for the cause.

"And the murder?" he asked.

"I don't regard my actions as murder."

"Lady Jane Grey."

"You think I killed her? Pushed her down the stairs? Why and where's your evidence, Doctor?"

I think she saw something you did or were doing, V.J. thought, but that's no evidence of murder. It will be for a Court to decide.

Dr Patel realised it was the best he could do. He'd exposed the offender and protected the lives of the remaining patients – if that's what all of them wanted – and the reputation of the Twilight Nursing Home.

However did he really agree with his actions? Not the exposure of course, you couldn't have people killing off others willy-nilly like wartime, but as had been argued why should you keep someone alive who wanted to die? What right had he as a doctor or

Reverend Lord as a minister of religion, well-educated people, to decide against the death of a labourer or a shop assistant who had reached a painful end to their life?

Uncomfortable as it was as a medical practitioner, it probably was time voluntary assisted dying, a death with dignity alternative to existing circumstances, was addressed legally.

Now to return to the present.

"The two policemen who have been investigating are in the next room and would like to talk to you. Would you like them to come in here or would you prefer to join them outside?"

There was no answer, then the click of the door closing.

In the silence which followed the weary but relieved voice of Robert Carroll intruded: "So now we need another hospital visitor."

EPILOGUE

The trial of Marion Turner took place in the region's ornate Victorian sandstone court house, well away from Drummond, which was deemed too partisan for a fair trial. Even a judge alone trial was decided upon, finding unbiased jurors thought to be too difficult.

Ms Turner pleaded not guilty and represented herself.

The case attracted more than curious locals. As V.J. had predicted it became a cause celebre.

People from near and far including Lois and Ben Blake, the prominent national advocate and high church officials attended. There were protest meetings for both sides and religious vigils outside the court house.

The national media followed the daily progress and the spirited defence of her actions by the ex-hospital visitor, supported by evidence under oath of all sub-poenaed committee members, that the dead patients had expressed the wish to die, drew both public admi-ration and criticism.

Petitions were drawn up by her supporters dem-anding action by the Federal government on death with dignity, euthanasia, mercy killing or voluntary assisted dying – a mishmash of well-intentioned means to allow those who wanted to, to die. An appeal was anticipated whatever the verdict.

The judge reserved his decision and returned to the State capital.

The Crown decided not to pursue the murder charge about Lady Jane Grey due to lack of evidence.

Marion Turner remained on remand.

Dr V.J. Patel, no longer anonymous, left Drummond with his secrets and moved several hundred kilometres further inland to continue to provide medical services.

And the 'public' jury still is out upon the overall issue of a choice in dying. Indeed, they've never been asked to reach a decision.

The End?

www.ingramcontent.com/pod-product-compliance
Lightning Source LLC
Chambersburg PA
CBHW022119280326
41933CB00007B/456